ALEXANDER
THE GREAT
THE LEGEND OF A WARRIOR KING

Greek peasants working in the fields

The people of Thebes appeal to the goddess Demeter to save them from Alexander's soldiers.

Greek hoplite

Alexander marrying a Persian princess

Ammon, Egyptian king of the gods

The city of Thebes under attack from Alexander's troops.

Scientists in Alexander's expedition

Members of the Macedonian army

ALEXANDER
THE GREAT
THE LEGEND OF A WARRIOR KING

Written by
PETER CHRISP

Illustrated by
PETER DENNIS

Macedonian soldiers

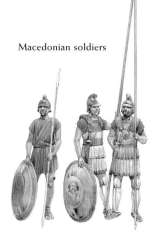

Alexander's
personal
historian and
secretary

A Dorling Kindersley Book

Dorling DK Kindersley

LONDON, NEW YORK, SYDNEY, DELHI, PARIS,
MUNICH, AND JOHANNESBERG

Project Editor Carey Scott
Art Editor Joanne Connor
Senior Editor Scarlett O'Hara
Deputy Managing Art Editor Vicky Wharton
Managing Editor Sue Grabham
Senior Managing Art Editor Julia Harris
DTP Designers Andrew O'Brien, Georgia Bryer
Picture Researcher Deborah Pownall
Jacket Designer Dean Price
Production Kate Oliver and Chris Avgherinos
US Editor Chuck Wills

First American Edition, 2000
00 01 02 03 04 05 10 9 8 7 6 5 4 3 2 1

Published in the United States by Dorling Kindersley Publishing, Inc.
95 Madison Avenue New York, New York 10016

DK Publishing offers special discounts for bulk purchases for sales promotions or
premiums. Specific, large-quantity needs can be met with special editions, including
personalized covers, excerpts of existing guides, and corporate imprints. For more
information, contact Special Markets Department, DK Publishing, Inc.,
95 Madison Avenue, New York, NY 10016 Fax 800-600-9098

Library of Congress Cataloging-in-Publication Data

Chrisp, Peter
   Alexander the Great / by Peter Chrisp
      p.cm. -- (Dorling Kindersley discoveries)
   Summary: Follows the history of Alexander the Great and his campaign to conquer
   the known world, including information on his traveling companions, armies of his
   time, ships, and food.
   ISBN 0-7894-6109-9
      1. Alexander, the Great, 356–323 B.C.—Military leadership—Juvenile literature. 2.
   Greece—History—Macedonian Expansion, 359–323 B.C.— Juvenile literature. 3.
   India—History--To 324 B.C.—Juvenile literature. 4. India—Discovery and
   exploration--Greek—Juvenile literature. [1. Alexander, the Great, 356–323 B.C. 2.
   Kings, queens, rulers, etc. 3. Generals. 4. Greece—History—Macedonian Expansion,
   359–323 B.C.] I. Title. II. Series.

DF234.2.C48 2000
934—dc21
                                                                                99-057736

Reproduced by Colourscan, Singapore
Printed and bound by L.E.G.O., Italy

Additional illustrations by David Ashby

see our complete catalogue at
www.dk.com

Contents

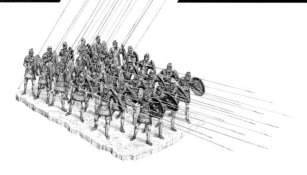

The Long Feud

I N ABOUT 500 BC, A SERIES OF WARS BEGAN BETWEEN TWO ANCIENT civilizations. Their dispute was to continue for almost 200 years. The conflict was started by the Persians, who were trying to expand their empire. Facing them in battle were their western neighbors, the Greeks, who were fighting to keep their freedom.

Persian soldiers wore trousers, tunics, and headscarves.

"Once we crush the Greeks, I shall pass through Europe from end to end and make it all one country. There is not a city or nation in the world which will be able to withstand us."

King Xerxes of Persia, quoted in Herodotus's book *Histories*, 5th century BC

This Greek vase, painted in the 4th century BC, shows King Darius I of Persia making plans for campaigns of war against Greece. In 492 and 490 BC, Darius made two unsuccessful attempts to conquer Greece.

The Greeks thought that naked men looked heroic, so in art soldiers were often shown fighting naked. In reality, Greek warriors wore body armor.

A 4th-century BC carving showing Greeks and Persians in battle

THE PERSIAN EMPIRE

THE ANCIENT PERSIANS AND Greeks were very different from each other. The vast Persian empire included many different people with various religions and languages. They were united in a single state, which was ruled by a king. In contrast, the Greeks all spoke the same language and worshiped the same gods, but were not ruled by one king. Greece was not an empire but a collection of city-states, which were like different countries with their own governments and laws. Some of the city-states, such as Athens and Sparta, were often at war with one another.

GREEK UNITY

In 380 BC, an Athenian politician called Isocrates called on the Greek cities to unite and invade Persia. Greece was a poor land, he said, which was why the Greeks were always fighting each other. But Persia was rich. All Greece's problems would be solved by conquering the Persian empire, and seizing its magnificent wealth.

The Parthenon in Athens was a temple to the goddess Athena. It replaced an earlier shrine burned by the Persians.

GREECE

CRETE

ASIA MINOR

• Sardis

• Miletus

Damascus

MEDITERRANEAN SEA

Jerusalem

River Nile

Thebes

EGYPT

RED SEA

Priest holding barsom

THE MAKING OF AN EMPIRE

The Persians were the ancient people of southern Iran. Between 549 and 522 BC, two Persian kings, Cyrus the Great and his son Cambyses, won a huge empire. It stretched from Egypt in the west to the borders of India in the east, and included some Greek settlements on the edge of Asia Minor. Later kings, such as King Darius I and his son Xerxes, hoped to expand the empire even further by conquering all of Greece.

Egyptian dwarf god Bes

ANCIENT MONUMENTS
The great pyramid tombs and the statue of the sphinx were already over 2,000 years old when the Persians conquered Egypt.

MAGI

The ancient Persians worshiped a supreme god called Ahura Mazda (wise lord), as well as other, lesser gods. Priests, called *magi* (from which our word "magic" comes), performed rituals to honor these gods. As he prayed, a priest held up a holy bundle of twigs called a *barsom*.

PERSIAN FINERY

The wealth, and the diversity, of the Persian empire was displayed in richly furnished palaces. Craftworkers of many nationalities made elaborate items, such as this silver bowl.

FACT file

• For almost 200 years, from about 522–334 BC, the Persian empire stretched 2,500 miles (4,000 km) from west to east.

• More than a dozen languages were spoken in Asia Minor alone.

• The great hall of King Darius's palace at Persepolis was big enough to hold 10,000 people.

"It is much more glorious to fight against the Persian king for his empire than to fight each other... We Greeks will never have lasting peace unless we join together."

Isocrates, from his speech given in Athens, 380 BC

XERXES

In 480 BC, the Persian king, Xerxes, came close to conquering Greece. He led a vast invasion force, which succeeded in capturing Athens and burning the city's temples. But the Athenians fought back and won a great victory. Xerxes had to flee back to Persia. The Greeks never forgave the Persians for burning their holy temples.

Illustration of King Xerxes of Persia, son of Darius I

SACRED FIRE
Persian priests, or magi, burned holy fires on large, open-air altars.

CASPIAN SEA

River Oxus

• Bactra

BACTRIA

Bactrian (two-humped) camels carried treasure across the empire.

Taxila •

Nineveh

ASSYRIA

P E R S I A N   E M P I R E

INDIA

River Indus

• Ecbatana

Darius I was the first Persian king to use the title the "Great King."

• Susa

The Ishtar gate was the entrance to the ancient city of Babylon.

WAR ELEPHANTS
Indian elephants were trained for war and used by the Persian army in their battles.

PERSIA

• Persepolis

PERSIAN GULF

ARABIAN DESERT

Assyrian citizen bringing a gift of fine cloth.

BRINGING TRIBUTE

Each New Year's Day, a great ceremony was held at the palace of Persepolis in Persia. People from all over the empire brought tribute (gifts) to the king as a sign of their loyalty. These carvings from Persepolis show Indians and an Assyrian bringing their gifts. The palace walls were covered with such carvings. They were intended to show the wealth of the empire and its many different peoples, all united under their Great King.

THE MACEDONIANS

NORTH OF GREECE LIES THE land of Macedonia. The ancient Macedonians spoke a form of Greek and worshiped the Greek gods. Despite this, other Greeks looked down on them as "barbarians," or backward foreigners. They thought that the Macedonians had rough, crude ways. Unlike the Greek city-states, which were mostly governed by the citizens themselves, Macedonia was ruled by kings. Between 359 and 336 BC, the king was a brilliant, ambitious man called Philip. When he came to the throne, his kingdom was small, weak, and surrounded by enemies. Philip created a powerful army, which he used to conquer the neighboring countries of Thessaly and Thrace, and to dominate the whole of Greece.

The hills of Upper Macedonia

On the plains, the farmers grew wheat and barley.

Macedonian women made bread at home.

Sheep were raised for wool and for milk, which was made into cheese.

HETAIRAI
Some women became trained companions called hetairai. They were taught to be witty speakers and skilled musicians. Hetairai often entertained the men at parties.

PARTY AT PELLA

When he was not away at war, Philip relaxed in his palace at Pella, where he often held drinking parties. This gave the Greeks another excuse to look down on the Macedonians – as drunkards. Greeks always mixed their wine with water, but the Macedonians were said to drink theirs undiluted.

These guests are playing "cottabos," a game in which wine was flicked at a target – here, a bowl on the floor.

Healthy living

LIKE THEIR GREEK neighbors, the Macedonians ate a simple diet based on wine pressed from grapes, bread made from barley or wheat, and olives – some eaten fresh, and others pressed for oil.

Rich and poor
The wealthy enjoyed seafood such as squid, and they hunted wild boar and deer for meat. The poor, however, rarely ate fish or meat.

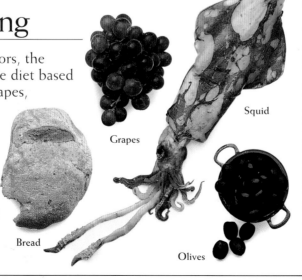

Grapes

Squid

Bread

Olives

HILLS AND PLAINS

Macedonia was a divided land. The plains of Lower Macedonia, where the king's rule was strongest, were occupied by people who spoke Greek. Upper Macedonia was hill country and home to tribes who spoke various languages. Philip's first achievement as king was to bring together all these different people into one kingdom.

Much of the land was wooded, and timber was sold to the southern Greeks for shipbuilding.

PLOWING AND HOEING

These farmers are preparing the ground for planting. One man steers a wooden plow pulled by oxen, while another man breaks clods of earth with a hoe. Most Macedonians were poor farmers, but under Philip's rule many of them became skilled soldiers, too.

PHILIP'S GOLD

In 357 BC Philip conquered Amphipolis, east of Macedonia. The region was famous for its gold mines, and Philip became the richest ruler in Greece. He used the gold to hire more soldiers, buy off his enemies, and to win over influential Greeks with bribes.

The palace floors were decorated with mosaics made from pebbles.

Philip was blinded in his right eye by an arrow during a siege.

> "Philip is no Greek... He is a filthy wretch from Macedonia, a place where it was never yet possible to buy a decent slave."
>
> Demosthenes the Athenian, from his speech *Third Philippic* 341 BC

A hired acrobat

Heating was provided by braziers – metal dishes containing burning charcoal.

A hetaira playing the aulos, *or double pipes.*

Philip's many slaves waited on him and his guests.

Macedonia today

For most of its history, Macedonia has been ruled by foreigners – Romans, Greeks, Bulgarians, and Turks. Following the breakup of Yugoslavia in 1991, Macedonia became an independent state again. It is much smaller than Philip's kingdom, and its inhabitants are not related to the ancient Macedonians.

PRINCE ALEXANDER

IN 356 BC, KING PHILIP OF MACEDON'S WIFE, Olympias, gave birth to a son, Alexander. The young prince soon learned that he came from an extraordinary family. Philip claimed descent from Heracles, the legendary strongman and son of the god Zeus. Olympias traced her bloodline back to the famous warrior Achilles. Tales of his heroic ancestors and news of his father's conquests filled Alexander with ambition. Whenever Philip won a victory, Alexander would complain to his friends, "Boys, my father will leave no great achievement for me to show the world."

OLYMPIAS
Prince Alexander was closer to his mother, Olympias, than to his father, who was often away fighting. Olympias was just one of the king's wives, and she bitterly resented her rivals. After Philip's death, she murdered his most recent wife and baby daughter. Alexander, like his mother, also had a ruthless streak.

Each string was tightened or loosened to produce a range of notes.

Stringed instrument called a lyre.

A musical life
Like every wealthy Greek boy, Alexander studied music as part of his education. He learned to sing and play the lyre, an instrument with a soundbox made from the shell of a tortoise. The strings were plucked with a disk called a plectrum. Music was played at almost every Greek social event, from religious festivals to private parties.

READY FOR ACTION
Alexander rushed to Craterus's aid, ready to attack the lion with his javelin.

The lion would adopt a defensive position as Craterus raised his sword.

WAR WEAPON
Alexander's friend Craterus is shown wielding a kopis, a curved sword used for slashing. The kopis and javelin were also used in warfare, so hunting was seen as a useful part of military training.

ROYAL SPORTS
Alexander and his friends are shown hunting a lion. Hunting was the favorite sport of the Macedonian royal family, and Alexander would have hunted almost daily. He stalked the wild animals, such as bears, lions, and stags, that still roamed the Macedonian hills.

ARISTOTLE

When Alexander was 13, the famous Greek philosopher Aristotle became his tutor. Aristotle was an expert in all the sciences as well as politics. Alexander came to share his tutor's curiosity about the natural world.

Education for girls

ALEXANDER'S SISTERS had a very different upbringing. They were taught to spin and weave wool into cloth. All Greek women, even princesses, were expected to spend their days at home, spinning and weaving.

1 The first stage in making cloth was to roll out the rough fibers into twisted strands. This was done on an *epinetron*, a pottery sheath that fitted over the knees.

2 Next, the wool was wrapped around a stick, called a distaff and spun into thread on a spindle. A spindle was a weighted rod of wood or bone.

3 Then the thread was woven into cloth on an upright loom – a timber frame resting against a wall. Even Queen Olympias would have had her own loom.

The ancient Greeks wore loose, simple clothes such as this dress, called a chiton.

A hilltop village

Alexander's servant ran to help.

ACHILLES
Alexander's hero is shown killing the queen of the Amazons, a legendary tribe of fighting women.

TAMING BUCEPHALUS
Alexander noticed that Bucephalus shied away from its own shadow. He tamed the horse by turning it toward the sun, so it couldn't see its shadow.

THE ILIAD

Alexander's ancestor, Achilles, is the hero of an epic poem called the *Iliad*. Composed by Homer some 400 years before Alexander's birth, the poem tells of a Greek war against Troy in Asia. When Alexander set off on his own Asian campaign, he took the *Iliad* with him, keeping it under his pillow.

THE FIRST FEAT

By his teens, Alexander was an expert horseman. His first recorded deed, at the age of about 12, was to tame a wild horse, Bucephalus, which nobody else had been able to mount. Over the years to come, Bucephalus would carry Alexander into the thick of many battles.

THE FIRST CHALLENGE

In 336 BC, King Philip of Macedon was at the height of his power. He had forced most of the Greek cities to join a military alliance, or league, headed by himself. The king planned to lead the Greeks in a war against the Persian empire. However, this plan came to nothing, because Philip was murdered. He was immediately succeeded by his son, Alexander, who was just 20 years old. When the news spread, there was a widespread rebellion against Macedonian rule. Alexander had to act quickly to save the situation. He had to prove that he was just as strong a king as his father had been.

Heracles
Alexander traced his family back to the legendary hero Heracles. The engraving above shows Heracles capturing Cerberus, the dog who guarded the underworld. Heracles was born in Thebes, one of the oldest and most famous of the Greek cities. Despite his link with Thebes, Alexander came to hate the city.

HAILING THE NEW KING
The soldiers proclaimed Alexander king by beating their spears against their shields.

KING ALEXANDER
The Macedonian throne did not automatically pass to the king's eldest son. First, Alexander had to be accepted by the army. On the very day that Philip was murdered, the soldiers hailed Alexander as their king. Alexander told them, "Nothing has changed except the name of the king!"

Alexander's soldiers poured into the city.

The soldiers' shields were decorated with a star – the emblem of the Macedonian royal family.

TRAINING FOR WAR
The Thebans, who had joined Philip's league, did not take Alexander seriously. In 335 BC, they withdrew from the alliance and surrounded the Macedonian garrison (supply of soldiers) that Philip had left in the city. The young men of Thebes began to train for a war with Macedonia, which they thought they would easily win.

NO SANCTUARY IN THEBES

When Alexander's soldiers stormed the city, frightened people fled to the temples, hoping they would be safe in such holy places. But the soldiers showed no mercy. They dragged people from the temples and murdered them. About 6,000 Thebans were killed during the battle.

As well as men, women and children were also sold into slavery.

HARSH PUNISHMENT

Alexander had the whole city burned to the ground as an example to the rest of Greece. A few noble Thebans who had opposed the revolt, plus the city's priests and priestesses, were spared. The remaining inhabitants, some 20,000 people, were sold as slaves.

IN HIDING
Some Theban soldiers hid from their attackers.

The terrified citizens tried to flee.

ESCAPE!
Mounted Theban troops fled to the countryside.

The city of Thebes under attack

Macedonian soldiers burst into houses, killing the occupants.

ATTACK ON THEBES

Alexander was away fighting in Thrace, to the north, when he heard that Thebes had risen in revolt. He raced south, covering 240 miles (386 km) in just 13 days. The Thebans were shocked to see Alexander's army so soon, but still they refused to surrender. A fierce battle followed, and the city was eventually taken by the Macedonian army.

MERCY GESTURE

A Theban woman called Timocleia killed one of Alexander's soldiers in self-defence. When she was arrested and brought to the king, he pardoned her. Alexander wanted to be seen as a merciful conqueror, so he made sure that everyone knew he had been generous.

THE GREAT EXPEDITION

ALEXANDER HAD CRUSHED ALL OPPOSITION IN GREECE. Now he planned a new war of conquest against the vast Persian empire. He said that it would be a war on behalf of all Greeks, to punish the Persians for invading their homeland 150 years earlier. He also intended to free the eastern Greek cities from Persian rule. By the spring of 334 BC, Alexander had gathered a huge army. It included not only Macedonians, but troops drawn from all over Greece and from the Balkan lands to the north. As well as soldiers, Alexander's expedition included scientists, architects, writers, artists, philosophers, and seers.

Wax tablet for taking notes

Eumenes, a secretary

Callisthenes, the historian

WRITERS

Alexander's secretaries wrote letters for the king and kept a diary of the campaign. For a more lasting record, Alexander had his own historian, called Callisthenes. "Alexander's fame," he boasted, "depends on me and my history."

ARTISTS

Poets, painters, sculptors, and musicians were among the artists who traveled with the king. Their role was to make statues and paintings of Alexander, and to celebrate his actions in poems and songs. These were all ways of bringing Alexander lasting fame.

Musician

Poet

Sculptor

ETERNAL FAME

Alexander's personal motive for the campaign was to win everlasting fame, and prove himself an even greater conqueror than his father.

A 16 ft- (5 m-) long sarissa, or pike

FIGHTING TROOPS

Alexander had two main cavalry units – the Macedonian companion cavalry and the horsemen of Thessaly. Most of the Macedonian infantry were foot companions. They fought alongside the Macedonian shield bearers, the fittest and toughest soldiers in the whole army. The expedition also included heavily armed Greek infantrymen called hoplites, archers from Crete, Balkan javelin-throwers, slingers, and Thracian scouts.

Shield bearers

Foot companion

12,500 Greek infantry

12,000 Macedonian infantry

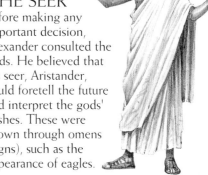

Aristander
the seer

MIND AND BODY

Alexander's personal physician was among a team of doctors. Philosophers gave the king advice and entertained him with their conversation.

Alexander's doctor, Philip of Acarnania

Anaxarchus of Abdera, a philosopher

BUILDERS

Surveyors, architects, and engineers were needed to lay out the army's camps and to build siege equipment, bridges and, later, whole cities.

Architect   Surveyor

THE SEER

Before making any important decision, Alexander consulted the gods. He believed that his seer, Aristander, could foretell the future and interpret the gods' wishes. These were shown through omens (signs), such as the appearance of eagles.

SCIENTISTS

The expedition was also a journey of exploration. Astronomers, map makers, and other scientists were on hand to record any discoveries. Geologists looked for valuable metals, such as gold.

Botanist

Geologist   Map maker   Astronomer

Pages   Groom

SERVANTS

Among the servants were grooms who cared for the horses and mules. The pages were noble Macedonian youths who served Alexander's meals, slept in his tent, and went hunting with him.

WOMEN AND CHILDREN

Some Greek women followed the army, and later on they were joined by many more Asian women. More than 10,000 babies were born during the campaign.

Soldier's woman and child

FACT file

● More Greeks fought against Alexander than served with him. The Persian king had a force of 50,000 Greek mercenaries (hired soldiers).

● Alexander left a second Macedonian army at home to prevent any further Greek uprisings.

● Callisthenes was one of several men on the expedition who wrote books about the campaign. Their accounts formed the basis of all future histories of Alexander.

Alexander's friend Hephaestion

Some shield bearers carried swords

Greek hoplites   Trumpeter   Foot companion officer   Slinger   Archer   Companion cavalryman   Thracian scout   Thessalian cavalryman

7,500 Balkan infantry

2,400 Greek cavalry

1,800 Macedonian cavalry

900 Balkan cavalry

A well-kept army

There were more than 37,000 fighting men in Alexander's army, and one of his biggest problems was making sure that every man received wages and food. The campaign began with enough grain to last just 30 days, so Alexander had to find new sources of food in Asia. He also needed to capture Persian treasure in order to pay his troops.

"Lord of all Asia"

A T THE CITY OF GORDIUM, IN THE TEMPLE OF Zeus, stood an old cart. Its yoke was fixed with a knot so complicated that nobody could undo it. According to a legend, whoever untied the knot would become "Lord of all Asia." Alexander could not resist this challenge. His brutal but effective solution was to slash through the knot with his sword.

Alexander drew his dagger to cut through the knot.

Renaissance wall-painting showing the story of the Gordian knot, painted in 1545–7 by Italian artist Perino del Vaga.

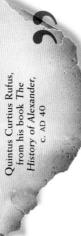

It was impossible to see where the knot began and ended.

Conquering Asia Minor
Alexander's victory at the Granicus gave him the freedom to lead his army through Asia Minor, from one Greek city to another. Most of the cities welcomed him, though two surrendered only after sieges.

THE BATTLE OF ISSUS

IN APRIL 334 BC, ALEXANDER LED HIS army into Asia Minor (present-day Turkey). In May, he fought a battle against the satraps, or local Persian governors, at the Granicus. Meanwhile, Darius III was far away in Babylon, collecting troops. It was not until late 333 BC that he marched north to Issus, and the two kings finally met in battle. The Macedonians were outnumbered by Persian troops, but Darius made a fatal mistake. He chose to fight on a narrow plain, where there was not enough room for his army, and thousands of soldiers had to wait behind the battlefront.

BATTLE WINNERS

Alexander was a better general than Darius, and his soldiers were very brave. The awesome Macedonian phalanx – a solid formation of infantry armed with pikes – mowed down the Persian troops. Meanwhile, Alexander himself led the cavalry charge.

The shield bearers were armed with swords.

Alexander was always first into battle, riding Bucephalus.

The shield bearers fought alongside the phalanx, protecting its unguarded right flank (side).

Swordmaking

ALL THE SHIELDS, helmets, and weapons used by Alexander's soldiers were hand-made by skilled smiths. Armor was beaten into shape from sheets of bronze. For spearheads and swords, iron was preferred because it is a much harder metal. Iron must be heated to a very high temperature – about 2,192°F (1,200°C) – before it can be worked.

1 The iron was heated in a charcoal fire until it was hot enough to be shaped.

2 For several hours, the hot iron was repeatedly beaten and reheated until it was the shape of a sword.

3 The sword was plunged into cold water to harden it, and then sharpened on a grindstone.

FORCE OF THE PHALANX
The men in the rear ranks pushed against those in front, making the force of the phalanx overpowering.

CAVALRY CHARGE

This ancient Greek sarcophagus (carved tomb), illustrates an episode from the battle of Issus. Alexander is shown attacking a Persian cavalryman. At Issus he made straight for Darius, but the Persian king fled. When news of Darius's flight spread, the whole Persian army began to retreat.

The length of the pike, or sarissa, allowed the phalanx to spear enemy soldiers from a safe distance.

Bronze helmet with cheek guards

Shield protected the soldier's left side.

Phalanx infantry were known as foot companions.

Greaves (shin guards)

FACT file

• 100,000 Persian soldiers, but only 450 Macedonians, were killed at Issus.

• During his campaigns Alexander was wounded at least ten times, by every kind of weapon, including swords, daggers, clubs, and stones.

Alexander's friend Hephaestion

Alexander is shown greeting his royal prisoners in a painting by Italian artist Sebastiano Ricci, 1708–10.

JEWEL OF ASIA
Darius's wife, Stateira, was said to be the most beautiful woman in Asia.

AFTER THE BATTLE

Darius fled from Issus in such a hurry that he left his mother, wife, and children behind. The women were terrified of Alexander at first, but he treated them with such kindness that they soon became fond of him. He would later marry one of Darius's daughters.

CONQUESTS

Just one year after defeating Darius at the battle of Issus, Alexander captured the major Phoenician port cities of Sidon and Byblos. They surrendered in 332 BC.

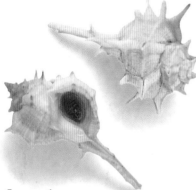

Sea snail

Tyre was one of the richest cities of the Mediterranean, thanks to a sea snail called the murex. These were crushed to make a prized purple dye, used to color robes and other garments. It took 60,000 sea snails to make one pound (half a kilo) of dye.

Carthage

The Phoenicians were an ancient seafaring people. They sailed all around the Mediterranean, founding trading cities. The most famous was Carthage, in today's Tunisia, which was founded by settlers from Tyre.

THE SIEGE OF TYRE

ALEXANDER HAD BEATEN DARIUS'S ARMY, but the Persians still had a powerful fleet of warships. While this fleet sailed the Mediterranean, Alexander would not be safe. He did not have enough warships to fight a sea battle, but he found another way to beat Darius's fleet. He planned to capture the ports that supplied the ships with food and water. Without supplies, the fleet would soon surrender. The first two ports gave up without a fight, but the people of Tyre resisted. They were sure that Alexander could be defeated, because their city was built on a well-defended island. Alexander's siege of Tyre lasted for seven months. It was his most difficult military operation, but he finally succeeded in capturing the city.

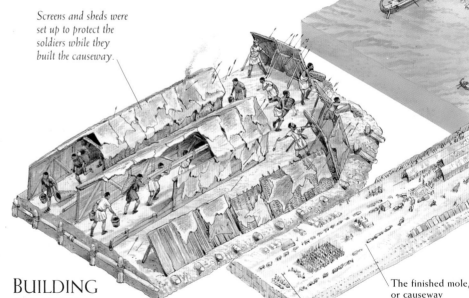

Screens and sheds were set up to protect the soldiers while they built the causeway.

The finished mole, or causeway

BUILDING A MOLE

Alexander ordered his men to build a mole – a land bridge – from the mainland to the island of Tyre. The soldiers drove wooden stakes into the seabed to act as a frame, and then piled rocks and logs on top. As they neared the city walls, the work grew more difficult and dangerous. The water was deep, and Alexander's men were bombarded with stones and fire from Tyrian catapults.

REACHING THE WALLS
The finished mole was about 200 ft (60 m) wide and half a mile (800 m) long. Unfortunately for Alexander, the wall facing the mole was too strong to be battered down. It would take an assault from the sea to do this.

BREAKING IN

Again and again, Alexander's ships, armed with battering rams, smashed against the city walls. Eventually, they managed to bring down part of the wall. Alexander then sent in troop-carrying ships with drawbridges attached. From these ships, the Macedonian shield bearers and foot companions fought their way into the city.

CATAPULTS

Both attackers and defenders used deadly catapults, which fired stones, red-hot lumps of metal, or bolts (big arrows). The catapults were fired by springs made from tightly twisted animal sinews or hair.

HOT SAND
The Tyrians tipped red-hot sand on top of Macedonian soldiers trying to climb the wall.

Tyrian soldiers filled their shields with sand, and then heated them over braziers.

A soldier aims the catapult.

CUNNING TRICK
Some Tyrians threw spears attached to ropes at their attackers' shields. They pulled on the ropes to force the Macedonians to drop their shields.

Siege engine

TACTICAL TOWERS
The Tyrians built wooden towers on top of their walls. These made it harder for the Macedonian catapult missiles to reach them, and gave their own artillery greater range.

The Tyrians piled rocks into the water to prevent Alexander's ships from getting close to the island.

VICTORY AT LAST

After months trying to capture Tyre, most of the Persian fleet surrendered in 332 BC. With these new warships, Alexander was able to attack Tyre from all sides. After the Macedonian victory, the adult men of Tyre were nailed to wooden crosses as a warning to other cities.

Pairs of ships were lashed together to provide a stable platform for the siege engines.

THE CITY OF ALEXANDRIA

FROM TYRE, ALEXANDER TRAVELED southwest to Egypt, the richest province of the Persian empire. The Egyptians hated Persian rule, and they gave their new conqueror a warm welcome. On November 14, 332 BC, the 24-year-old Macedonian was crowned pharaoh, or king, of Egypt. Alexander spent six months in his new kingdom. While he was there he made plans to build a great port on the Mediterranean. He chose the site and named the city Alexandria. This was the first of 17 cities that Alexander named after himself.

A GOOD OMEN

Alexander scattered barley on the ground to mark out a plan of the city's streets, but was alarmed when most of it was eaten by birds. However, Aristander, his seer, said that this was a good sign, because it meant the city would attract many settlers who would be well-fed.

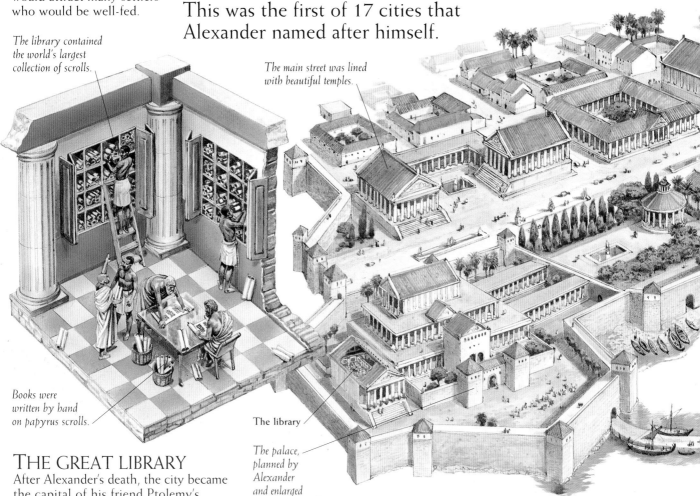

The library contained the world's largest collection of scrolls.

The main street was lined with beautiful temples.

Books were written by hand on papyrus scrolls.

The library

The palace, planned by Alexander and enlarged by later kings.

THE GREAT LIBRARY

After Alexander's death, the city became the capital of his friend Ptolemy's kingdom. Ptolemy founded a great library in Alexandria, and gave orders for copies to be made of all the world's books. The library became famous, attracting scholars and scientists from many lands.

AN ALPHABETICAL CITY

By the early third century BC, Alexandria was a flourishing and, for its time, modern city. It was settled by Greeks, Jews, and Egyptians, each living in their own neighborhoods, named after letters of the alphabet. The Jews, for example, lived in Delta (the Greek letter D).

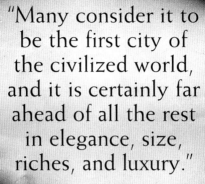

"Many consider it to be the first city of the civilized world, and it is certainly far ahead of all the rest in elegance, size, riches, and luxury."

Diodorus of Sicily, from his book *The Library of History*, 1st century BC

Son of Ammon

ONCE HE WAS CROWNED PHARAOH, Egyptian priests greeted Alexander as the son of Ammon, their most important god. This made a deep impression on Alexander, who had always felt that he was no ordinary human being.

Horns of Ammon
After Alexander's death, coin portraits were made, showing him wearing the ram horns of Ammon.

King of the gods
Alexander believed that Ammon was Zeus, king of the gods, under a different name. He was shown wearing a crown decorated with two goose feathers, or sometimes with a horned ram's head.

This Egyptian pharaoh holds a crook and flail to represent kingship.

Living god
As a pharaoh, Alexander was worshiped by the Egyptians as a living god. Nobody knows if Alexander really believed that he was a god, but he certainly enjoyed being treated as one.

A Greek theater

The agora, or marketplace

GRID SYSTEM
Alexandria had a network of straight streets at right angles to each other, like many cities of today.

The garden of the royal tomb, or soma

The Pharos lighthouse

The eastern, or Great harbor. The western harbor was called the Harbor of the Happy Return.

A causeway linked a little island called Pharos to the mainland.

WONDER OF THE WORLD

In 279 BC, a lighthouse was built on the island of Pharos. It was 400 ft (122 m) high, and so solidly built that it stood for more than 1,000 years. The lighthouse was proclaimed as one of the seven wonders of the ancient world.

Alexandria today
Aristander's prediction proved correct, because today Alexandria supports a thriving population of around three million people. It is the second largest city in Egypt, and is still the country's chief port. For more than 2,300 years, merchant ships have sailed to and from the city's harbors.

" Everything you possess is now mine...If you wish to dispute your throne, stand and fight for it and do not run away. Wherever you may hide yourself, be sure I shall seek you out."

Alexander, in a letter to Darius, 331 BC

)arius, surrounded v Macedonian kes, was frozen horror as exander charged vard him.

Darius's charioteer whipped his horses furiously to speed his master's escape.

A 1st century AD Roman mosaic showing Alexander and Darius in battle. The mosaic was copied from a Greek painting of about 300 BC.

Clash
of two Kings

ALEXANDER HAD MET DARIUS IN BATTLE ONCE BEFORE, AT Issus, when the Persian king fled in terror. Determined not to be beaten a second time, Darius spent two years gathering a new army before he was ready to fight again. This time, the prize for victory would be the whole Persian empire.

Alexander is shown spearing a Persian nobleman.

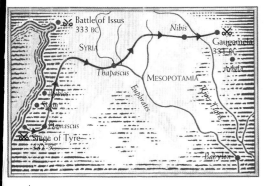

Battle of Issus 333 BC

Journey to Gaugamela
Alexander left Egypt in the spring of 331 BC and traveled back to Tyre to gather his troops, now around 47,000 men. In the summer, they marched northeast, reaching Gaugamela in late September.

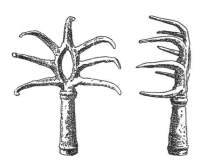

Offerings to the gods
Before battles, animals were sacrificed to the gods in order to win their help. Sometimes special hooks such as those above were used to pull the flesh back and reach the inner organs. Marks on the organs were believed to be omens (signs) from the gods, showing how the battle would turn out.

THE BATTLE OF GAUGAMELA

DARIUS HAD TWO YEARS TO FIGURE out why he had lost at Issus and to plan for a second battle. Alexander had won the first time with a cavalry charge, so Darius strengthened his own cavalry with his empire's best horsemen.

APPEAL TO FEAR

For the first and only time in his life, Alexander sacrificed an animal to the god Phobos (Fear). In his prayers, he asked Fear to fill the Persians with terror during the coming battle. Alexander knew he needed all the help he could get to defeat the massive Persian army.

BATTLE OMENS
The seer Aristander held a ram's liver. He told Alexander that the omens indicated a victory for the Macedonians.

The Macedonian camp

Macedonian troops marched to the battlefield.

A STIRRING SPEECH

Before the battle, Alexander made a rousing speech to his men. He reminded them of their previous victories, and told them not to worry that they were outnumbered. "There may be more men *standing* on their side," he said, "but there will be more *fighting* on ours."

Soldiers for hire

ALEXANDER CLAIMED to be fighting for all of Greece, though many Greek mercenaries (hired soldiers) fought in Darius's army.

Fighting for Persia
By Alexander's time, Greek mercenaries had fought for Persia for more than a century. Greece was a poor land, and it was hard to make a decent living at home. Persia was a rich empire, and the king always needed soldiers.

He had new weapons of war, too. There were
15 elephants from India to terrify Alexander's horses, and
200 chariots with razor-sharp blades sticking out from their
wheel axles. This time, the Persians would outnumber Alexander's
men by five to one, and Darius would not repeat the mistake of
fighting on a narrow, crowded battlefield. Instead, he looked for an
open space, where he could use all his forces. In September 331 BC, he
found what seemed the perfect place for the battle – a wide open
plain near a village called Gaugamela (in modern-day
Iraq). He led his huge army from Babylon to
Gaugamela, and waited
for Alexander.

The Persian camp

*The vast Persian
army streamed down
on to the battlefield.*

CHARIOT CHARGE

The 200 Persian war
chariots charged across
the plain. Alexander's archers
and javelin throwers attacked them,
bringing down the drivers and horses.
When the chariots reached the Macedonian lines, the
soldiers opened their ranks, letting them pass through.

CAVALRY BATTLE

The battle began with hard fighting
between Alexander's cavalry and
Darius's Scythian horsemen. Heavily
outnumbered, the Macedonians lost
many men. But they managed to
hold off the Scythians until
reinforcements arrived.

GROUNDWORK

Darius had prepared the battleground carefully. In some
areas, his soldiers had scattered metal spikes called
caltrops to cripple the Macedonian horses. Other
areas had been cleared of obstacles and the ground
leveled to give the Persian chariots a smooth ride.

THE IMMORTALS

Darius had a personal bodyguard of 10,000 specially chosen soldiers called Immortals. They received this name because when one of them was killed, he was immediately replaced by a new recruit, so that it seemed that the soldiers defied death. This frieze (flat sculpture) of Immortal soldiers, armed with spears and bows, comes from Darius's palace at Susa.

The village of Gaugamela

BATTLE TROPHIES
After the battle, the Macedonians marked their great victory with trophies – these included Persian arms and armor, stripped from the dead and displayed on poles.

Nineveh, an ancient Assyrian city already in ruins by Alexander's day.

Alexander thrust his spear at Darius's driver.

Hephaestion's gashed arm was cleaned and bandaged.

HEPHAESTION WOUNDED

Doctors were stationed behind the lines ready to tend to the injured. Alexander's closest friend, Hephaestion, was wounded when his arm was slashed by a spear. Hephaestion was probably treated by Alexander's personal physician, Philip of Acarnania.

THE TURNING POINT

Darius's fatal mistake was to leave a gap in the Persian line of defense. Alexander at once led his companion cavalry through the opening, and galloped towards Darius himself. The two kings faced one another. Alexander was able to kill Darius's chariot driver before the Persian king leapt from the chariot and fled the battlefield in a cloud of dust.

TOO LATE

Alexander rode through the night to reach Darius, but was too late to catch the king. Although Alexander was disappointed, he knew that Darius was now a broken man. Alexander had beaten the best army the Persians could raise, and on a battlefield chosen by Darius. Now nothing could stop him from becoming ruler of the Persian empire.

Alexander gazed in wonder at the Persian king's treasures.

THE KING'S TREASURE

In Arbela, Darius had abandoned his treasure. Thanks to these riches, Alexander was able to reward his soldiers with vast amounts of loot. Meanwhile, Darius had escaped by fleeing east through the mountains to the land of Media, where he gathered the survivors of the battle.

ARBELA
Darius's base was the town of Arbela, 60 miles (96 km) from the battlefield.

FAST PACE
Alexander's cavalry traveled more than 400 miles (644 km) in just eleven days.

IN PURSUIT

The following spring, Alexander gathered an army of 9,000 men and set off once more in pursuit of the king, who was now heading northeast. It was a long, exhausting chase.

Darius was carried off in a covered wagon.

Betrayed

Darius hoped to fight Alexander again, but his satraps, or governors, had lost faith in his leadership. Led by Bessus, satrap of Bactria, they plotted to overthrow their king. In July 330 BC, Darius was taken prisoner by his own men. He was tied up, flung into the back of a wagon, and taken into the desert by Bessus and his friends.

IGNOBLE END

When they realized Alexander was close behind them, Darius's captors decided to kill the king. Two of them dragged Darius from the cart and stabbed him repeatedly. By the time Alexander reached them, Darius was dead. Alexander gave his enemy a royal funeral at the Persian capital, Persepolis.

Babylonian welcome
Alexander made a triumphant entry into Babylon, riding his chariot. To welcome their new king, the Babylonians scattered flowers on the road in front of him. Alexander promised to rebuild the city's temple to the chief Babylonian god Bel Marduk, which had been destroyed by the Persians. This made him very popular with the Babylonians.

A NEW GREAT KING

THE PERSIAN ARMY HAD BEEN UTTERLY defeated on the plain at Gaugamela. Now Alexander was free to take the prizes of his victory. These included Babylon and Susa, two rich and ancient cities that had been conquered by the Persians. Their inhabitants surrendered at once to Alexander, and they welcomed their new ruler. After several weeks resting in Babylon, Alexander traveled southeast into the land of Persia and towards Persepolis. There was no welcome here. Any Persians who did not flee fought to defend their homeland, but they were soon overwhelmed. At the age of 25, Alexander had become ruler of the Persian empire – the new Great King.

Stone lions stood guard at either side of the hall.

The hall columns were 59 ft (18 m) tall.

The Persian palace of Persepolis

The chief Persian god, Ahura Mazda, shown as a pair of outstretched wings.

Frieze of royal guards, called Darius's Immortals

FACT file

- Alexander captured five of Darius's royal palaces, at Babylon, Susa, Persepolis, Pasargadae, and Ecbatana.
- Darius's treasure was enough for Alexander to pay his army for 25 years.
- The treasure weighed around 7,290 tons.

A 14th-century Armenian painting of Alexander

ON THE THRONE

When Alexander first sat on the Persian throne, Demaratus, an old Greek soldier, wept with emotion. He said that any Greek who had died before that day had missed one of the greatest pleasures of life – seeing Alexander on the throne of Darius.

THE EMPIRE'S WEALTH

For years, each district of the Persian empire had paid taxes to King Darius. Gold and silver were brought by camel to his palaces. When Alexander became the Persian king, there were so many valuables in the palaces that 20,000 mules and 5,000 camels were needed to carry them to the new king's treasury at Ecbatana.

PALACE OF PERSEPOLIS

In January 330 BC, Alexander entered the great palace of the Persian kings at Persepolis. It was an awe-inspiring building. At its center was a vast "apadana," or audience hall, where the Persian king sat on his throne and received visitors from all over his empire.

Gold and silver

ALEXANDER FOUND THE PERSIAN PALACES full of gold and silver. He was not interested in the treasure for its own sake, and much of it was melted down to make coins to pay his troops.

Silver ornaments were melted down into coins called drachmas.

Gold armlet decorated with mythological animals.

Royal goat
This silver goat may have been an ornament in one of Darius's palaces.

Armlet
This solid gold armlet, or bracelet, was once worn by a Persian noble, perhaps the king himself.

PALACE IN RUINS

After staying in Persepolis for four months, Alexander burned the palace down. He claimed that this was done to punish the Persians for burning Athens in 480 BC. However, some said that Alexander was drunk at the time of the fire and later regretted destroying his palace. Persepolis was abandoned. All that remained were the stone doorways, carvings, and palace columns.

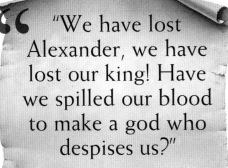

PLOTS AND QUARRELS

FROM 330 UNTIL 327 BC, ALEXANDER campaigned along the northeastern frontiers of the Persian empire, fighting against a series of local rulers. It was here that he began to fall out with his Macedonian followers. Hoping to be accepted as king by the Persians, Alexander had begun to wear Persian dress and to welcome Persian nobles into his court. He expected the Macedonians to treat his Persian friends as equals and to bow as the Persians did when they greeted him. The Macedonians hated the new Persian courtiers, and they refused to bow. They felt that Alexander had become arrogant. Now, he was even claiming to be a son of the god Zeus. The Greeks saw their king changing for the worse, and they did not like it.

A burning torch was held to Philotas's face.

LISTENING IN
From behind a curtain, Alexander listened to Philotas being tortured.

PHILOTAS'S PLOT

As relations with his Macedonian followers grew worse, Alexander began to suspect plots against him. In 330 BC, he was told that Philotas, who commanded the companion cavalry, was planning to murder him. Philotas was arrested, tortured until he confessed, and executed. Historians still argue about whether or not Philotas was guilty.

PAYING RESPECT

Alexander's Persian nobles were used to bowing in front of their king while blowing him kisses, an act of respect known as *proskynesis*. To Macedonians, such gestures were made only to statues of gods. When Alexander demanded *proskynesis* for himself, they felt he wanted to be treated like a god.

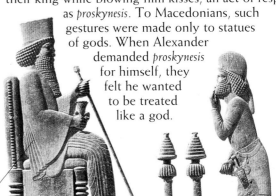

The Persian king Darius I on his throne, receiving proskynesis.

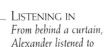

HEAVY DRINKER

Alexander was a heavy drinker, like his father Philip. He would often spend several hours drinking wine with his friends and then stay in bed for the whole of the next day, recovering from his hangover. Alexander had always had a bad temper, but it was made much worse by wine.

A cup called a kylix, *commonly used at drinking parties.*

MURDEROUS INTENT
A nearby guest tried to hold Alexander back when he realized the king was about to murder his friend.

In a moment of drunken fury, Alexander had killed Cleitus.

FATEFUL FRIENDSHIP
Cleitus was the brother of Alexander's childhood nursemaid and had once saved the king's life. But this did not prevent Alexander from killing him.

Both Cleitus and Alexander had drunk too much wine.

THE KILLING OF CLEITUS

During a drinking party, one of the older Macedonians, Cleitus, began to criticize the king. He said that Alexander's father Philip was a better man than he would ever be. Alexander, who was drunk, lost his temper, and ran Cleitus through with a spear.

Hero or devil?

ALEXANDER HAS ALWAYS been seen in different ways by different people. Some have seen him as a brutal killer, while to others he is a noble hero.

Two horns

Coins showing Alexander wearing the ram's horns of the god Ammon led to a later belief that he really had horns, like a devil. In the Muslim holy book, the Koran, he is called "Dhul Quarnein" – the two-horned one.

A 16th-century Persian miniature showing Alexander as the "two-horned one."

Alexander's head is surrounded by a halo.

Indian king

This 15th-century painting from India shows Alexander leading the luxurious life of an Indian emperor of the time.

Victory in India

IN 326 BC, ALEXANDER LED HIS army into India to begin a new campaign of conquest. His first battle was against the Indian king Porus, whose huge army included more than 100 elephants, specially trained for battle. Although Alexander's army was outnumbered, his tactics, and the discipline of his men, eventually won the battle.

King Porus, said to be over 7 ft (2 m) tall, rode an elephant. From its back he hurled javelins at the Macedonians.

Alexander riding into battle on his faithful horse Bucephalus.

Shortly after the battle, Bucephalus died from either wounds or old age.

Shield bearers hacked at the elephant's legs with axes to cripple them.

Dead and dying elephants littered the battlefield.

The Defeat of Porus by Alexander by French artist Louis Watteau was painted in the mid-18th century.

"Porus, gathering forty beasts around him, drove at the enemy with the whole mass of his elephants and inflicted grevious losses."

Diordorus of Sicily from his book *The Library of History*, 1st century BC

Victory coin
Alexander marked his victory over the Indian king Porus with this silver coin. It shows Alexander on Bucephalus attacking Porus mounted on an elephant. After the battle, Porus became a useful friend to Alexander.

INTO AN UNKNOWN LAND

WHEN ALEXANDER LED HIS ARMY INTO India in 326 BC, he was setting off on a journey into the unknown. The Greeks had only vague ideas about the size, the climate, and the people of India. Alexander believed it was a small country that would be easy to conquer. However, the Indian ruler Porus told him that large powerful kingdoms lay ahead, defended by huge armies including thousands of elephants. This alarming news spread through the Macedonian army. His soldiers began to wonder whether they would ever see their homes again.

> "You are always busy and up to no good, traveling so many miles from home, a nuisance to yourself and to others."
>
> Indian wise man, quoted in Arrian's *The Campaigns of Alexander,* c. AD 150

Unfamiliar fruits looked tempting, but often led to sickness.

Soon, the soldiers' wet clothes started to rot from the constant rain.

June 326 BC | RAINY SEASON
Alexander invaded India at the start of the summer rainy season – the worst possible time of year. For two months, it rained continuously. The rivers burst their banks, flooding the surrounding plains.

April 326 BC | WORDS OF WISDOM
Alexander had a famous meeting with some Indian wise men who spent their time thinking about the world. They told him that his life of conquest was senseless. They stamped their feet to make the point that a person can only possess the earth that he or she stands on.

A NEW TOWN
On the site of his victory over Porus, Alexander founded two cities called Nicaea (Victory) and Bucephala. The latter was named in honor of his faithful horse, who died following the battle.

Medieval French painting showing the building of Bucephala.

Indian treasures

ALEXANDER TOLD his men that they would find rare treasures in India, a land rumored to be rich in precious stones.

Strange birds
The soldiers saw animals and birds they had never seen before, including peacocks. Alexander ordered his men not to kill the beautiful birds and peacock feathers were sent back to Greece.

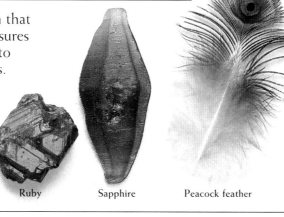

Ruby   Sapphire   Peacock feather

Ancient skill
Alexander's men built floating bridges across some of the Indian rivers by lashing together boats and fixing planks of wood over them. Supplies and horses could then be brought across. This ancient method of building bridges is still used in the Punjab today.

MAKESHIFT BOATS
The soldiers stuffed their tents with straw to make rafts, so they could float themselves and their belongings across the river.

CROSSING RIVERS
July 326 BC

Alexander led his army through the region called the Punjab, which means "land of five rivers." The soldiers crossed four of the rivers, which were swollen and fast-flowing because of the heavy rains. Some of the men were swept away by the strong currents.

NO MORE HARDSHIP
July 326 BC

When the soldiers reached the fifth Punjab river, the Hyphasis, they refused to cross it. Their spokesman, Coenus, told Alexander that the men wanted to go home. "The one thing a successful man should know," he told Alexander, "is when to stop!"

MISERABLE LIFE
June 326 BC

The rains were a continual source of misery. All the metal equipment had to be scoured daily to keep it free from rust. Deadly snakes came out of their holes in the ground looking for higher, dry land. Many men died painfully of snakebites.

Crocodiles added to the danger of crossing the Indian rivers.

The soldiers gathered outside Alexander's tent, begging him to give up the campaign.

DEFEATED
Aug 326 BC

Alexander was furious with his soldiers, and announced that he would go on alone if necessary. When this failed to change their minds, he sulked in his tent, refusing to speak to anyone for three days. At last, Alexander gave in, and told his men that he would take them home.

THE JOURNEY HOME

ALEXANDER'S SOLDIERS WERE OVERJOYED WHEN he agreed to lead them home. But their sufferings were far from over. Instead of returning the way they had come, Alexander decided to continue exploring, following the Indus River south to the Indian Ocean. The army would have to fight their way toward the coast, against the most warlike people of India. Then the expedition would separate, with Alexander leading his followers across a vast desert. More soldiers were to perish from hunger and thirst during the desert crossing than had died in all the battles in Asia.

THE ROUTE

After traveling down the river, Alexander divided his army into three. Craterus took the oldest soldiers to Carmania by an easy, northern route. Nearchus, with the fleet, was ordered to explore the Persian Gulf. Meanwhile, Alexander led the bulk of the army through the Gedrosian desert.

Indus River

Craterus's route

Gedrosian desert

Alexander's route

Carmania

Nearchus's route

Susa

Persian Gulf

Dec 326 BC — SETTING OFF

Alexander's carpenters built a great fleet of ships for the journey down the Indus River, and on into the ocean. They worked so hard that the fleet was ready in just two months.

There were 80 30-oared galleys.

The horses traveled in flat-bottomed barges.

Feb 325 BC — FIERCE WARRIORS

The army traveled through the lands of the ferocious Mallians, who lived in strongly defended towns. Alexander captured one town after another. During one attack, he was almost killed when an arrow pierced his lung.

TRAIL OF DESTRUCTION
Alexander's army burned villages, massacring or enslaving the local people.

Sep 325 BC — TOUGH JOURNEY

While crossing the scorching desert, Alexander was brought a precious drink of water by one of his scouts. The king thanked him, but poured the water away. Alexander showed that he was willing to share the

Alexander indicated that he would suffer along with his soldiers.

*The starving soldiers killed their horses
and mules and ate the meat raw.*

*The sick and exhausted were
left behind to die in the desert.*

STRANGE PEOPLE

Oct
325
BC

On the coast, the army came
upon tribes of fish-eaters who
lived in huts made from whale and fish
bones. They lived on a diet of raw fish,
which they tore up with their clawlike
nails. The Greeks were shocked by the
fish-eaters' wild appearance.

SEA MONSTERS

Nov
325
BC

In the Indian Ocean, a school of whales began
to follow the fleet. The sailors were terrified.
They had never seen whales before, and thought they
were monsters. Nearchus ordered his men to blow
trumpets and shout, and the whales fled at the noise.

REUNITED

Nov
325
BC

After 60 terrible days
crossing the desert,
Alexander reached safety in
Carmania. With the arrival
of Craterus's troops and
Nearchus's fleet, the army
was reunited.

A mass wedding

ALEXANDER CELEBRATED
his arrival in Susa
with a mass wedding.
More than 90
Macedonian officers
took Persian brides,
including Alexander
himself. The king
hoped this would win
him Persian support.

Shipbuilding

USING SIMPLE TOOLS,
Alexander's carpenters built
a fleet of about 2,000 ships.
They constructed both river
craft and seaworthy vessels.

Basic tools
The chopper was used for chopping
down trees and hacking wood, the
saw for cutting rough planks, and
the adze for planing surfaces.

Chopper

Saw   Adze

Alexander's funeral carriage

DEATH IN BABYLON

IN BABYLON, ALEXANDER MADE plans to conquer yet more territory. He intended to invade Arabia and then conquer the whole coast of North Africa. However, at the end of May 323 BC, the king fell ill with a raging fever. From his sickbed he continued to give orders about the coming campaigns, but his fever grew worse. It soon became clear that Alexander was dying. His friends asked him, "To whom do you leave the kingdom?" The king replied, "To the strongest," but he could not know who this would be. Alexander knew only that his generals would soon be fighting each other for power. His last words were, "I foresee a great funeral contest over me." On 10 June, Alexander died. He was just 32 years old, but he had conquered the greatest empire the world had ever seen.

The carriage had a roof of overlapping gold scales.

Statue of Nike, goddess of victory

Bells warned onlookers of the procession's approach.

Net of fine gold thread

Panels painted with scenes of Alexander's wars

Columns decorated with acanthus plants

The gates of Babylon

FUNERAL PROCESSION
Alexander's soldiers marched behind the carriage.

ROYAL CARRIAGE
The Macedonians spent an entire year preparing a magnificent funeral carriage to carry Alexander's body home. As it traveled westward, the fame of the carriage spread. In every city, vast crowds gathered to watch the dead king's procession pass. But Alexander's body never reached Macedonia. The carriage was seized by Ptolemy, the new ruler of Egypt, and taken to Alexandria.

A life at war
Alexander spent almost all of his 13-year reign at war. He was one of the greatest generals in history, and won dozens of battles and more than 20 sieges, yet he also found time to build around 20 cities.

TWO KINGS
After Alexander had died, his wife Roxane gave birth to a boy. Alexander also had a half-brother, Arrhidaeus, who was mentally handicapped. These two were proclaimed as joint kings, though they never had the chance to rule. All Alexander's relatives were murdered in the power struggle that followed his death.

THE BABY KING
Alexander's son, King Alexander IV, was murdered, with his mother, when he was twelve years old.

356 BC	334 BC	333 BC

ALEXANDER BORN IN PELLA, MACEDONIA.	ALEXANDER INVADES THE PERSIAN EMPIRE.	ALEXANDER DEFEATS DARIUS AT THE BATTLE OF ISSUS.

Banner decorated with a golden olive wreath

THE CONQUEROR

After Alexander's death, rival Macedonian warlords fought one another for a share of the empire. The largest territory was seized by Seleucus, who was nicknamed "the conqueror." His Seleucid empire, which included Persia and Syria, lasted for 241 years.

Seleucus

Ptolemy

LAST DYNASTY

Ptolemy was the most fortunate of Alexander's successors. Unlike Seleucus, who was assassinated, he lived into old age. Ptolemy founded the last dynasty (family of rulers) of Egyptian pharaohs, the Ptolemies, who ruled Egypt from 305 to 30 BC.

The king's armor was placed on a purple robe.

Jars of sweet-smelling spices surrounded Alexander's body.

Golden lions stood guard in front of the coffin.

Sixty-four richly dressed mules pulled the carriage.

The Hellenistic world
The period after Alexander's death is called the Hellenistic age (from the word Hellene, which means Greek). For 300 years, Greek language, art, and culture flourished throughout the Middle East. A typical Hellenistic city was Ephesus (above) in Turkey.

Legacy of Alexander
The Kalash people of Pakistan believe that they are descended from soldiers in Alexander's army who married local women. The customs, language, and religion of the Kalash are unlike anything else found in Pakistan, so this story may be true.

332 BC	331 BC	327 BC	323 BC
SIEGE OF TYRE. ALEXANDER CROWNED PHARAOH OF EGYPT.	BATTLE OF GAUGAMELA. CITY OF ALEXANDRIA FOUNDED IN EGYPT.	ALEXANDER INVADES INDIA.	ALEXANDER DIES, POSSIBLY OF MALARIA. 

EMPIRE BUILDERS

THROUGHOUT HISTORY, new empires have been conquered by military might. Some, such as the Roman empire, were well-organized and long-lasting. Others had only a brief lifetime before breaking up into separate states or kingdoms. In successful empires, the conquered people have been united by a shared religion, language, or way of life.

MAP SHOWING THE ROMAN EMPIRE IN AD 117

The Roman world
At its largest extent, the Roman empire stretched from Britain to Asia. Troops were kept busy guarding the frontiers of conquered lands. The heart of the empire was the Mediterranean, which the Romans called "our sea."

JULIUS CAESAR

THE ROMAN EMPIRE
The Romans allowed many of the people they conquered to become Roman citizens and to share in the benefits of their empire. This made the Romans popular rulers.

Maker of the empire
Julius Caesar (c. 100–44 BC) was one of a series of generals who created the Roman empire. Caesar conquered Gaul (France), and he dreamed of equaling the achievements of Alexander the Great.

Standards, emblems representing Roman army units

Trajan's Column
Under the Emperor Trajan (AD 98–117), the empire reached its largest size. His campaigns in Dacia (present-day Romania) are recorded in a series of carvings on a pillar, known as Trajan's Column, still standing in Rome. Above, Roman standard-bearers (soldiers carrying emblems) lead other troops across a bridge made of boats.

Roman roads
The Romans built an extensive network of roads all over their empire in order to move soldiers quickly around conquered lands. Roads were built in straight lines to keep the distance between places as short as possible. The first Roman road was the *Via Appia* (left), built in 312 BC and later extended to become Rome's main link with its expanding empire in the East.

Gift of the empires
The Roman and Islamic empires each left a lasting legacy. Most of the countries conquered by the Arabs are still Muslim. The Romans left behind the Latin language and calendar. Some European cities, such as Paris and London, were founded by the Romans. The Mongols left no long-term legacy.

300	200	100 BC	0	AD	AD 100	200	300
				THE ROMAN EMPIRE			
270 BC: ROME CONTROLS ALL OF ITALY.	197–146 BC: CONQUEST OF MACEDONIA AND GREECE.			AD 43: CONQUEST OF BRITAIN.	AD 117: ROMAN EMPIRE REACHES ITS LARGEST SIZE.		337: EM SPLITS I TWO.

THE ISLAMIC EMPIRE

In the 7th century AD, a new religion, called Islam, appeared in Arabia. Its founder, the prophet Muhammad, united the tribes of Arabia, and inspired them to fight a holy war against their neighbors.

United by religion

Most of the conquered peoples converted to Islam. They were called Muslims, and they followed a strict code for everyday life. Muslims pray five times a day, often in mosques (prayer buildings).

MAP SHOWING THE ISLAMIC EMPIRE IN AD 850

The Muslim world

By AD 850, Muslim armies had conquered territory from Spain to the edge of India. The capital of the Islamic empire was Baghdad, which was a great trading center and the world's largest city.

Holy decoration

Another unifying force was Arabic, the language of the Muslim holy book, the Koran. Texts from the Koran were often used as decoration in Muslim buildings. This inscription comes from Cordoba in Spain.

Genghis Khan

The founder of the Mongol empire was Temujin, who took the title Genghis Khan ("prince of all that lies between the oceans"). He claimed that his god, Tengri, had given him a mission to conquer the world.

THE MONGOL EMPIRE

In the 13th century, the fierce Mongols from Asia conquered the largest land empire in history. For almost a century, Mongol armies seemed unstoppable. Yet, although they were brilliant warriors, the Mongols did not have the Roman or Arab skill for ruling people.

MAP SHOWING THE MONGOL EMPIRE IN AD 1259

MONGOL WARRIOR'S QUIVER (CASE FOR ARROWS)

The Mongol world

Genghis Khan united the Mongol tribes and led them in an invasion of China and Persia. His successors conquered southern Russia. At its peak, the Mongol empire stretched from eastern Europe to the Pacific Ocean.

Mongol weapons

The Mongols' success was due to their military tactics. They were expert horsemen and skillful with bows and arrows. Always ready to learn new skills, the Mongols may have been the first people to use gunpowder in war.

Mongol decline

In 1259, Genghis Khan's grandson Kublai was the new Great Khan, but his power never reached far beyond China. In the 1270s, Kublai made two attempts to conquer Japan, but each time his fleets were destroyed by typhoons. The Mongols no longer seemed invincible.

THE MONGOL FLEET SAILS TOWARD THE SHORES OF JAPAN

400	500	600	700	800	900	1000	1100	1200	1300

THE ISLAMIC EMPIRE

THE MONGOL EMPIRE

400–450: WESTERN EMPIRE FALLS TO NORTHERN BARBARIANS.

634–650: CONQUEST OF SYRIA, PALESTINE, IRAQ, EGYPT, AND PERSIA.

909: EMPIRE IS SPLIT BY A RIVAL GROUP OF MUSLIMS.

1237–1242: MONGOL ARMIES SWEEP THROUGH RUSSIA, POLAND, AND HUNGARY.

DISCOVERING KING PHILIP'S TOMB

Little remains from the lifetime of Alexander the Great. Even our statues of the king were made long after he died, copied from earlier statues that have now been lost. So it was exciting news when Greek archaeologists announced, in 1977, that they had discovered a rich tomb in Macedonia. The tomb held the bones of a man, along with symbols of royalty. This was evidence that the man was a king. Objects found within the tomb date from the fourth century BC. It was almost certain that the tomb was that of Alexander's father, King Philip of Macedon.

Unnatural bumps and hollows in the ground can give an indication that buildings once stood on the site.

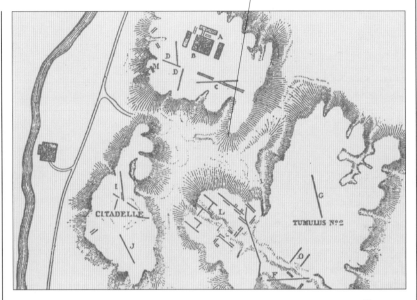

SITE PLAN

1 MAKING A SITE PLAN

Archaeologists look for features on the ground, such as tumuli (earth mounds), which are often the sites of ancient burials. Philip's tomb was found under just such a mound. Once a suitable site has been identified, a plan is made of the area before digging begins.

2 SPECIAL TOOLS

Archaeology is painstaking work, requiring delicate tools. To reach Philip's tomb, the archaeologists had to carefully move tons of soil, which they then sifted for finds. Small fragments of pottery in the soil were used to date the burial of the tomb.

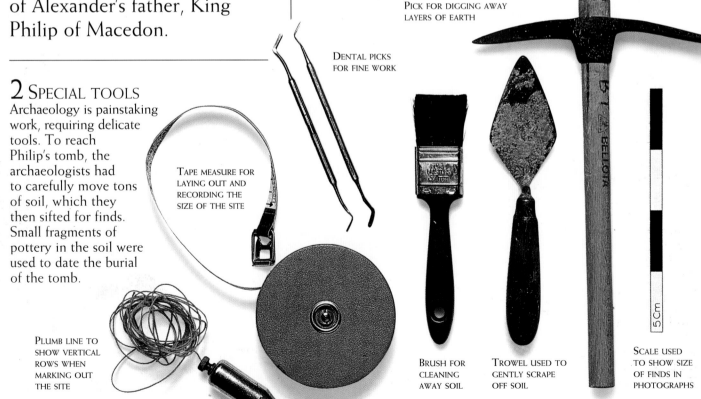

PICK FOR DIGGING AWAY LAYERS OF EARTH

DENTAL PICKS FOR FINE WORK

TAPE MEASURE FOR LAYING OUT AND RECORDING THE SIZE OF THE SITE

PLUMB LINE TO SHOW VERTICAL ROWS WHEN MARKING OUT THE SITE

BRUSH FOR CLEANING AWAY SOIL

TROWEL USED TO GENTLY SCRAPE OFF SOIL

SCALE USED TO SHOW SIZE OF FINDS IN PHOTOGRAPHS

5Cm

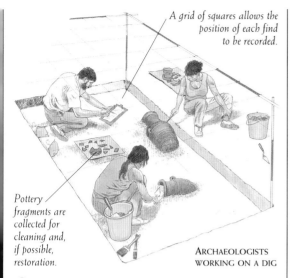

A grid of squares allows the position of each find to be recorded.

Pottery fragments are collected for cleaning and, if possible, restoration.

ARCHAEOLOGISTS WORKING ON A DIG

Rebuilding Philip's face

ALTHOUGH THE BODY buried in the tomb had been cremated, there were enough pieces of the skull left to reconstruct the dead man's face. A plaster cast was made of the skull, and clay was used to build up the layers of muscle and skin.

The shape of the beard was based on portraits of Philip.

RECONSTRUCTION OF KING PHILIP'S HEAD

The wound
An exciting discovery was a notch on the skull's right eye socket. Its angle showed that it was a wound caused by a blow from above. We know from accounts of Philip's life that he lost his right eye to an enemy arrow.

3 DIGGING THE SITE
Excavating a site often means destroying its evidence, preserving only finds, such as bones and treasure. It is important for archaeologists to measure, examine, and record even small finds. They take photographs and keep site notebooks in which they record the position of their finds.

4 THE TOMB
The king was buried with a magnificent set of armor, including a quiver and gilt leg greaves (coverings). Unlike most ancient royal tombs, Philip's grave had never been robbed. The armor was found in 1977 exactly where it had been placed at Philip's funeral in 336 BC; perhaps by Alexander himself.

Tiny, delicately crafted olives

GOLD OLIVE LEAF WREATH

5 WREATH
Gold wreaths such as this one have sometimes been found in Macedonian and Greek tombs. They were modeled on different types of leaf, and each leaf was linked with a god. The olive tree was sacred to Athena, while the oak was Zeus's holy tree.

Larnax
After his body had been burned, King Philip's bones were carefully wrapped in a purple cloth. They were then placed, with his wreath, inside this gold larnax (ancient Greek casket). The larnax was then put inside a marble sarcophagus (coffin) for extra safekeeping.

The lid was decorated with a starburst, the emblem of Macedonia's royal family.

GOLD LARNAX

Rosettes inlaid with blue glass paste

Index

Acknowledgments

The publisher would like to
thank:
Janet Allis for visualizing The
Siege of Tyre, Polly Appleton and
Sheila Collins for design
assistance, and Chris Bernstein
for the index, and Arbour
Antiques.

The publisher would like to
thank the following for their
kind permission to reproduce
their photographs:
Picture credits:
t=top, b=below, l=left, r=right,
c=center

AKg London: 8l, 8t, 11c, 21tr,
32tl, 35tr, 43c, 45tl. Ancient Art
& Architecture Collection: 13br.
Bridgeman Art Library,
London/New York:
Archaeological Museum,
Thessaloniki, Greece/ Bridgeman
Art Library 47br; British Library,
London, UK/Bridgeman Art
Library 38bc; Louvre, Paris,
France/Bridgeman Art Library
30tr; Musee des Beaux-Arts,
Lille/Lauros Giraudon/Bridgeman
Art Library
36-37; Museo Archaeologico
Nazionale, Naples,
Italy/Bridgeman Art Library 43tl;
National Archaeological
Musuem, Athens, Greece/

Bridgeman Art Library 14br;
Persepolis, Iran/Bridgeman Art
Library 34br. British Museum,
London: 2tr; 8br, 12cl, 25tcr,
33cr, 33tr, 41bl, 47b. Cambridge
University Museum of
Archaeology and Anthropology,
Cambridge: 44c. Corbis UK Ltd:
9tr; North Carolina Museum of
Art 21br; Ric Ergenbright 39tr.
E.T. Archive: 12tl, 13tl, 25tc,
32cl, 35br, 38tl, 44c. Mary
Evans Picture Library: 44bl.
Sonia Halliday Photographs:
16bl, 22bl, 33br, 43tr.
Robert Harding Picture Library:
6, 9b, 9br, 25cr, 43cr, 47cl.
The John Hillelson Agency:
Roland and Sabrina Michaud

35bl. © Michael Holford: 13bl,
33c. Hutchison Library: 11br.
Kostas Kontos: 47cr.
Manchester Museum: 47tr.
Soprintendenza Archeologica,
Naples: 7tr. Scala: 18-19, 26–27.
Telegraph Colour Library: 25br.

Additional photography:
The Museum of Archaeology
and Anthropology, 45cr; Geoff
Brightling, 45cl; John Heseltine,
44crb.

Jacket:
British Museum: front cover left,
back cover left. Sonia Halliday:
front cover centre. © Michael
Holford: front cover bottom.